SHITTING ON ELVES

&

OTHER POEMS

✷

SHITTING ON ELVES

&

OTHER POEMS

✺

LOREN GOODMAN

&

PIROOZ KALAYEH

NEW MICHIGAN PRESS
DEPT OF ENGLISH, P. O. BOX 210067
UNIVERSITY OF ARIZONA
TUCSON, AZ 85721-0067

<http://newmichiganpress.com>

Orders and queries to <nmp@thediagram.com>.

Copyright © 2020 by Loren Goodman & Pirooz Kalayeh. All rights reserved.

ISBN 978-1-934832-75-2. FIRST PRINTING.

Design by Ander Monson.

Cover illustration by Jeffrey Brown.

## CONTENTS

This is a Study of Human Nature  1
In the Catbird Seat  4
The Morning is of the Essence  6
Eckhart Tolle  7
Robert Downey Jr.  10
Poem About Math  12
My Edits  15
Your Edits  16
If We Were More Than We Are Snow  17
If We Were Cess  19
No Thing Can Be Everything  21
Dancers in the Dark  22
Hope Sells  24
Being Beijing  27
Peanut Poem  29
Morning  31
Being Another  34
On Rain  36
Film Crew  37
On Verde  42
On Verde II  44
5 Minutes to Midnight  46

*Acknowledgments*  53

*For the Elves*

# THIS IS A STUDY OF HUMAN NATURE

This is a study of human nature
When I pursued myself
Beyond the typical lines of pursuit

My hands—the first signs
My feet—the last
Ordered together in a perfect "I" formation
The perfect ego
Like a note sung long ago
By a chocolate cherry songstress
In the middle of my life

A crisis of humanity
Can begin the same way
Which is to say
I am in a perfect state of crisis
But I don't let it bother me

Scrolling down helps
Those who help themselves
While the generous reveal secrets
Beyond the typical lines of pursuit

What do I now know of nature?
Little more than I know of myself
The beating of my heart, the

Passing of blood and air through my lungs,
Reminds me that if nothing else
I barely notice anything, even though I'd like to think otherwise

Perhaps this is the wisdom of nature
This not knowing in the middle of crisis
At the wheel of a cherry-red Chrysler Avenger
Down Chestnut and Maple
Kids in the trunk
And the Phillies about to win the pennant
And the elephant is about to eat a peanut
And she shuts off her tablet and looks at me and says
"Many people have asked about you."

My hands and feet are still in perfect formation
My ego still intact
I clear my throat—twice.
Because I do everything twice
I eat twice as much as I should,
Half as much as I could
Explain myself in a way that could be scrolled away

The kids in the trunk
Are listening now
To The Who
I windmill on the steering wheel. She
Reminds me of myself
Tugging at her bottom lip.

The entire population of Holland
Could be stoned and eating frites, but I'd still be in the
 doghouse
Pursuing my lips
Beyond the typical lines of pursuit

## IN THE CATBIRD SEAT

In the catbird seat
I sit, waiting
For a sign

If I were more patient
I could design a new
Dime, one with a portrait
Of the world the way
I want it and a portrait of
The person who put me here:
Mrs. Ellis, my first grade teacher
Who taught me to say "apple"
But I am not that patient

Instead, I look over my laundry
List of complaints. High on the list
Is my forehead; towards the middle
My dissatisfaction and hatred
Of all of humanity, and last but
Not least, second-hand smoke

If I were more patient, I could
Check in to the local hospital
And make a real difference
Or at least a real diffidence

I would make rounds with
My complaints and a heart-
Shaped balloon for anything
Real to help me forget about
My expanding gut and…

Moral of the story:
All goes onward, nothing collapses
Nothing falls apart

## THE MORNING IS OF THE ESSENCE

The morning is of the essence
Solid states of man made intuition
Eggs sizzling in oil
Freeway above us
Freedom below us
My father, visiting, puts his hands
Above him like he's just won
A gold medal while the chef turns
Up the heat I contemplate a rose
Petal stem and leaf, thorn and iris
Gertrude Stein and inner silence
"Do you remember that movie?"
My father asks. "The one where
He says, 'FREEDOM!'" Yes—
We all remember the movie
"Mel Gibson," I say. *"Braveheart"*
"No," Mad Max replies, "Me give
Mel son!" I pick up the kid and Dad
Makes a motion to hand him over
Perhaps this is the essence of emotion
Contradictions and reversals of fortune
Eggs sizzling in oil
As Marlon Brando once said,
"I could have been a container."
And that has made all the difference

## ECKHART TOLLE

Eckhart Tolle
Is your friend
Oprah Winfrey
Is your enemy
Jay-Z
Is your DJ
Dr. Oz
Is your entropy
Edvard Munch
Is home alone
Macaulay Culkin
    Is friends with Elijah Wood
Fred MacMurray
Is an unknown entity
Dennis the Menace
Was a show we watched
In black and white
Michael J. Fox
Is Alex P. Keaton
Val Kilmer
Is Jim Morrison
Janis Joplin
Is friends with R. Crumb
Aline Kominsky
Is an exclamation point question
Mark in underground comics

Batman & Robin Williams
Don't necessarily go together
Charles Dickens
Was a serialized author
Charles Manson
Is not allowed to appear
In this poem
Kurt Cobain
Remains known
For his suffering
Unabashedly disciplined and driven
A sonic shifter between the sheets
Tennessee Williams
Had a secretary and love
Companion named Frank Merlo
Frida Kahlo
Was played by Salma Hayek
Who was also played by herself
When she stood up for women's
Rights in Hollywood she was
Standing up for the story of me
The story of anyone who has been
Made other or smaller than the sum of their hearts
Anyone who takes center stage in the theater of the now
In the fifth floor auditorium of W16 in Daejeon, Korea
In the fifth floor auditorium of my head
Three images in front of me
Future, present, past

Free objects from the force of gravity
Free radicals from the fears of sanity
Indicators of a phenomenon
Known as Billy Dee Williams
Aka Mother Margarine Pearl-Off
A dear old friend of Major Tom
And Gremlins
But I know it was always better when
Girls were boys
And Michelangelo drew circles in the sand

Suddenly you take one step back
And realize that art is this simple
And that what arises is of no importance
Names and names upon names
Yours truly,
Robert Downey Jr.

## ROBERT DOWNEY JR.

The other day, a homeless person asked me
For spare change in 7 different languages
I was so impressed, I gave him an eighth

"No tengo dinero," I said,
Cupping my warm hands through
Thousands of cold gold coins

"I am bigger than Jesus," I thought
"I am Iron Man." I walked to a bodega
And got a curry wrap
Not your typical sandwich
It was slathered in yellow-white
Mayo and had a big hunk of
Lettuce right down the middle

I yanked out the lettuce
And threw the rest on the floor
The homeless guy stooped to pick it up
A different homeless guy
One who spoke only five languages

I held up my hand, as
If to say "five languages?"

"Not a chance in hell," I thought
"Not even any Nepalese"

"Did I ever tell you about my
Trip to Nepal?" he replied

"I am bigger than Jesus,"
I said. "I am Iron Man."

"That reminds me of my trip to Nepal"

I held up my hand
But it was no longer there
My legs
My knees
My elbows
Were, however, present.

The homeless guy held up his hand
In some uninterpretable gesture

I got Jeeves on the console for consultation
I like Jeeves, he resolves my discombobulation

Then it hit me like a ton of small rectangular objects:
"I am not a scientist. I do not know quantum physics"
For which Jeeves prescribes Squanto's analgesics

## POEM ABOUT MATH

Most of my friends are numbers
43, 38, 26, 73, 19
Boom—you won the lottery

So I have a lot of friends now
Most of whom, as I said, are numbers
What I really like about numbers

Is what I really like about friends
You can put them together
Subtract them, multiply, divide

They can be rational
Or irrational, variables
Or become infinite

Even imaginary!
My first imaginary number
Came in darkness

I was practicing word problems
For four hours a day
At a secondhand desk

On the second floor
Of our apartment in
Lawrenceville, New Jersey

When I suddenly realized:
This is not math
This is love

Moreover, I have come
To understand that 1+1
Equals inequality

That numbers are often
At odds with one another
For the sake of their own

Perseveration: this
This is how words can suddenly
Help us fill up a loss

Orwell said 2 plus 2 is 5
Dostoevsky said 2 times 2 is good
Nietzsche said 1 divided by 1 does not exist

And yet despite all the odds
Or, rather, along with them
I find such pleasant evens

And it is the combination of these
The ways in which they gather
And associate, as if at a party

With Steven, that renews
My faith in, if nothing else
Myself = fraternity

**MY EDITS**

Everything I say sounds like spaghetti
On a white shirt
Or Picasso reading a Robert Frost
Porno—all the words
I say from the way
You look at me
And think of falling
Or going to Virginia
And taking the kids
And telling me things:
"I'm not attraction to you anymore."

Well, I could do the same
I could choose this tie
This way to hold you
Before myself

## YOUR EDITS

On the other hand
At times, when I am less critical
I simply don't know what to say
That is to say
What was once said
By the famous editor
Walter Murch who talked about how
"Houdini's job was to create a sense of wonder,
And to do that he didn't want you to punch here"

## IF WE WERE MORE THAN WE ARE SNOW

Falling, we are more than ever
Which is to say, a lot more than flakes

Past the archeology of the present
Digging through space like Galileo
Digging through dirt like John Henry
Digging through air like Amelia Earhart
Digging through ears like Ali Baba Q-Tip
Dragging memory through mirrors
To place us together in a frame: the entire
Junior Varsity Hunchback of Notre Dame

Here, relationships are easier
Test-tube babies
Taking the heat
Only costs $10K per try
A pack of Schwarzeneggers ready to kill
With a complimentary Petri eye
And a bucket of chicken crisps
If Danny Devitro shows up

We'll all smoke in the lavatory
Goose each other on a night on the town
Drink whole milk and watch drive-in movies
Juggle gizzards and guzzle the future
It doesn't make a difference
Because it is the difference it wants to be

That's how the imaginary works
And how the caged bird sings:
"THE BIRDS, of all Note, Plumage, and Degree,
That float in Air, and roost upon the Tree;"
Are all that were ever in thee

## IF WE WERE CESS

We'd sell for less
'Cause cess don't play
Or sell at Payless—but
If it did, the world would be lighter
More aerodynamic
Like a jumbo jet

My thoughts would also be lighter—
But not allowed on board

Simplicity requires less baggage
As does soaring above the clouds

Just imagine, if you will
A plane full of passengers empty of thoughts

They are on their way to Bermuda
But it is not the triangle that matters

Each passenger can see this as clearly
As the gremlin on the wing

We feel neither fear nor longing
For we view the gremlin as belonging

Just another one of us, our vision
Just another dream surgeon's incision

Surety, insurance and reinsurance
Coffee, tea or milf

## NO THING CAN BE EVERYTHING

My latest slogan
A slow gun held by a
Hotshot = hot to trot
Then I get zaftig
Eat a whole bag of chips

Would life be better
With or without the chips?
Is it possible to stop?

I softly wonder
About nothing

When others whisper about nothing
I think about you

That's my new slogan
Hope it sells

## DANCERS IN THE DARK

Can feel things others can't
With this new hardware you can
Also ask a question at the speed of thought
And become an international pedant

Ticks can occur if water is applied
"Just do your rain dance!" the shaman cried
I was lying down as he drummed around me
My eyes zooming in and out on the zombified

Is it just me? Or are these the first drops of rain
A sound like television but more like a rocket
Division cuts the spine of America
In every drop a light
Grass grows silently

Walt Whitman snores
On the cot above me
Rimbaud, Verlaine, and Baudelaire below
Smoking corn cob pipes azaleas in bloom
Each burning in the night
Of the rain-soaked room. Meanwhile,

The shaman calls for all to "Stay grounded!"
Upon his steed, drumbeats pounded
While doubt sits waiting for greed to make up its mind

Whitman's apnea cured, leaves of grass refined
These machines as bright as coffee grinding
Bitter-sweet gears of beans the body unbinding
Shadows interlaced like cotton fields on a plantation
Like Van Gogh and Chubby Checker
Dance-discussing depression
Through the wordless language of the twist
Sadness can function as a shield
Against feelings of hope and desire
As madness can suction Alka-
Seltzer elves through barbed wire
Some say this is the end of all downpour
And it is why, throughout history,
Writers have been so good at perpetuating it.

## HOPE SELLS

My name is Candy
Friends say I'm the next Kenneth Goldsmith
Others say Kenneth Goldsmith's the next me

My second grade teacher, Mrs. Ellis, said I'd be a congresswoman
My art history professor said Candy was a prostitute's name
I say tell that to the candy companies

Now I adjunct for four different schools
I'm single, overweight, and I've got a kid from a teenage marriage
And I'm here to tell you about life under sea

Some of you might think that this course is just about coral reefs
Protecting marine wildlife, and petting dolphins—well, you're
Absolutely right!

"It says here we're going to have to do a weekly journal."
Well, you can forget about that
So...uh...my name is...uh...
Did I tell you my name?

A middle-aged woman knocks on
The open door to the classroom
She is dressed in black face and
A maid's uniform like something
Out of *Gone With the Wind*

I know what you're thinking
Well, this woman is all of us
"But what does this have to do with marine wildlife?"

Aram Saroyan pokes his head
In the classroom the clock ticking a wave crashing
His name is Aram
He's right on time

And he asks: "Is this the conceptual pottery symposium
On Vanessa Place and her misappropriation of black face?"

Please take a seat back there
That's right
Behind Ron

Behind Ron?
Sorry, I don't sit behind Ron
First of all
Ron is 7 feet tall
If I sit behind him
I'll see nothing at all
Second of all
He farts like a madman!

The point of the conceptual is in the thinking.
Besides, Ron isn't really that tall, now is he?

Are you saying his height is in my mind?

It could be
Our thoughts are often farts that betray us
As are our Rons

Aram smiles like he did when he first slapped
Jack Kerouac with Ted Berrigoogle back in the day
Hopefully Aram doesn't mind the fart that I'm overweight

Suddenly, everyone's phart begins ringing all at once with the same ringtone

Loren Goodman and Pirooz Kalayeh, who are seated inside one another
Look down at their phones to read this identical text:

*Bonjour! Je suis Jacques Cousteau, ici avec Jimi Hendrix.*
*Personne ne meurt jamais! Nous sommes tous ici, au fond de la mer.*

## BEING BEIJING

Many of you have doubtless been to China
The future as it is called in the corporate marketplace
But most of us here are concerned primarily with the past
As archaeologists, it is all that matters, and all that will ever matter
Which is why I have invited you here today to become
　Archaeologists
Of the Future!!

Please take the neural helmets below your seats and attach them
　now
We are scheduled to arrive in Beijing in ten minutes

Those of you who have brought your pets for mind melds are now
　welcome
To attach cathode ray tubes

Remember our primary directive: removing the "JI-" from
　BEIJING

Please also don't forget to forget

That's funny—I often feel our society has forgotten about the
　importance of forgetting
When we were children, we may have foraged for memories of
　previous incarnations

I am here to tell you we can be children again
We can claim the future as the past, forget again
Or we can simply, slowly chew sassafras


In Kuala Lumpur and Saas Fee, we have Doctors
Scheldt and Muelheimer standing by to input your pass codes
Those of you who have forgotten yours can get by with crazy knees
The rest of you can now to begin erasing the letter J as well as any memory of Kareem Abdul and his various associates: Magic, MJ, Ricardo Montalbán, Geraldo, Francesco Clemente, and sexual semiotics
All prophets and pioneers of Being
Sending love in the form of serapes
Frida and Chihuahuas
Llamas and Ali Babas
Fall between these intercontinental sagas
Rising like galaxies between Carl Sagan's nalgas
Such is the architecture of Chinese puzzles
Such is the space where the solemn nose nuzzles

## PEANUT POEM

Begins as it should
Line by line
Word by word
Touching
Herds
By the tip of each trunk

While magic multiplies under
Each nutty crunch
Savory punch
Bunched together
Rows upon rows
Like ladles through crystal
Maids through dark matter
Polish tusks unbrittle
Drip painting splatter
A Pollack pancake riddle
Over and over again

One is brown on both sides
A natural outgrowth of a need
Or so consciousness confides
Using sticks and hardened brushes
And cultivated in the valleys of tushes
Harvesting occurs in two stages

First and foremost, peanuts
Second and segundo, words
Third and thirstily,
Swizzle Gillespie

Each tone through his horn
Pyretical sphinxian geometries
An interactive voyage through time in three dimensions
Cheeks puffed full
Six notes repeated
A spiral structure from the inside out

Jimmy Carter undefeated
Hungry for lunch
George Washington Carver whipping up some brunch
Slaving away with the sun bearing down

## MORNING

Bluebird on my shoulder
Blackbeard on my lap
Fingers snapping joy
And all that crap

People get upset if you're too chipper these days
Give me two dozen with the wood chipper glaze

That's my path forward
That's my way back
That's why I say:
I'll always be black

Like this Samsung keyboard covered in dust
We all do that which we think we must

Some people in Seoul wear masks
Because they must; others try
Them on to prevent yellow dust
But you & I wear masks for other reasons
Your rainbow dream sway
Is a mask for all seasons
Now let's be more like Satchmo
Devout and pure, but still streetwise

Like the first American morning
Through George Washington's eyes
Cherry tree with the wood chipper glaze
Now myth me into mechanical cushions
Proof! There you is.

Stare, strain, steer, or stow
As every action doth bestow
A collision of particles to show
Boat scrimshaw hambone slapdown
He's got lots of kisses and money to spare
Giant malt liquor and a chocolate éclair
Delaware never looked so fair!

So kiss me and smile for me
The morning is alive with horns
And a farewell to arms & bells
Like the first morning
I'm too chipper to be stuck in this maze
A cloud getting rained on by another cloud
Wooden teeth with no glaze
Doing Jimi Hendrix proud
My foot on the bow and my hand on the now
Bee flies out of my penis as I take it out to pee
Then a dandelion, mistletoe, and honey suckle

I remember all my life
Raining down as cold as ice
Up the Potomac to Little Hunting Creek

The speed, the timing, the technique
Horseback riding, fox hunts, fishing, and cotillions
Whatever you think will earn you bazillions
The future of the nation
Rests in how you rise each day
So get on up—rise up, arise!
On the right side—up! The
Right side of your head

## BEING ANOTHER

Person is not as easy
To be another animal
Even harder. In any
Case, I am here to tell you
How it's done: rent BLACK
BELT JONES—not the
Movie, the man. This is
STEP ONE. STEP TWO:
Order pizza, vegetarian with
Extra cheese, this contains
Calcium, which is good for
The knees. Then call your
Friends for a movie party
STEP THREE: consider
What it means to have friends
If you are in a circle, don't jerk
STEP FOUR involves theater
And haberdashery; picture Sanford
Meisner in the role of Fred Sanford
And you will have some idea of
What this means. Then take any
Leftover thread and stitch up the
Beans. Twist in and out of each
Other's legs to the tune of *Sanford
& Son*. If you are a Stanford alum
You are welcome to be your own son

If not, you're welcome to be
A bum, or strip down to your
Red-hot poker mad crazy sun-
Shine of a Wallace Stegner
Fellow by the name of
Dr. A. Zul, former vice-Chairperson
Of the People's Republic of
Chairs believes in messages
From beyond the blue lagoon
Believes in the realms of the unreal
And the children who inhabit them
Each psychological force of a thousand
Quadrants beyond the light of my scepter
STEP FIVE: cut everything out
Cut out your tongue, your mind
Your elbow, your lice
Drip before you dry
And before you flip
Let one rip
Then sing the Star-Spangled Banner
With a look of wonder, with beer
On your knee and friends inside

STEP 6: repeat STEPS 2
Through 5. STEP 7: the
Final step and most cumbersome
Of all: step lively!

## ON RAIN

I love rain
It wipes the nose of civilization
So end my meditations
On rain

## FILM CREW

Monster and smokes and grumbles and cables
'Tis the spirit of production this madness enables
Come Kardashians, Brad Pitts and tan bitterness
Yet my primary purpose is not to discuss this

My aspirations are in contrast with lenses
Lined up like sheep to be or not to be
Mishandled—I guess that's why they call me
Scintillating; and so we move on
Past the Palmdale desert to Arizona and
John Ford and better days without
Dinosaurs or heroes to avenge

Just imagine *Jurassic Park*
Directed by John Ford!
Or *Star Wars*, for that matter
John Wayne or Henry Fonda
As the lead, wagons and Comanche
The Red Rocks in the distance
Horses bouncing and dust
John Wayne as Darth Vader
Henry Fonda as T Rex
Kim Kardashian as Chewbacca
Chewie as a Kardashian
Brad Pitt as Han Solo

Such is the balancing act
For Mr. Ford and friends
Kind of like walking upside-
Down on a balance beam
Or holding a frame long
Enough to see the sunset
The man both in and out of
The system, who looks at Kurosawa and says:
お前の映画をよく見とるで！

Which could mean, "You sure like rain!"
But we digress past sunsets and romantic notions
Frozen daiquiris and coconut lotions
A world of plutonium and apocalyptic scares
Of false bazookas and thinning hairs
Mixed into a devoted stare of a child
Looking forward in 1920 by 1080
To find meaning beyond USA
And Lafayette, Indiana, cornfields
And Scooby Doo; you break-a-da
Rhyme, da rhyme break you to
Another child in NYC who likes
Trains but doesn't realize it
Stands devoted to his mother and
Motherhood in general
Discusses pugilism and trains contenders
Chases tail and makes adversaries
But films it nonetheless

I step outside
Away from all the hubbub
My health issues, the phone calls
I think: how do I start my day?
As usual: 600 pushups
That is, if I were Iron Man
In the background I can hear
The sound of pure iron ore
I let this wash over me like
Reality television and I'm the star
Until the moment I realize
I am taller than most of the actors
Who play super heroes
Indeed, at 7 foot 3, I am a foot
Taller than Christopher Reeves
I push harder in my training
Refine my dance moves
Strap on the toe shoes
Apply some new lubes
I can make it here there and
Everywhere altitude
Approximately 30,000 feet
In a small shack in Nepal
In front of a short stack of pancakes
I find meaning in the words
Of the silent sherpas beside me
Who I have hired as a crew
Of the cinematographic spirit

We start our days together
And end our nights apart
No one mentions *Variety*
Or tells me who is down or what
We are a simple crew, these sherpas
And me, blended, a single entity
That is why the world
We live in disappears when
We eat Nepalese pancakes
Or drink horchata or sing a
Hymn or turn and clap to
The rhythmic gyrations of
Betty Sue, or find comfort in stars
Upon stars I'd never see in Los Angeles
My hands above me, my feet below
In an explosion of yellow and red Melrose
We suppose is Moses come to tell us again
To take the time to smell the noses
Of Yul Brynner or Charlton Heston it
Matters not, for we are one in the same

Approximately 30,000 feet
In a small shack in Nepal
From an olfactory perspective
Or an old factory directive:
WASH YOUR HANDS
CUT THE CHEESE
WEAR A HARD HAT
PROTECT YOUR JIMMY

The noodles in a bowl on the floor
The title of my last film
A pre-make of *Tampopo*
I found while talking to sherpas
In the desert of my underwater mind

Meanwhile, back at the ranch
The two of us sit and chaw with
John Ford and Akira Kurosawa
East and West
Yeast & Zest
Keats and Shield
Shelley and Byron
Katie, Lord Alfred and Telly
Savalas set up the grill
Talk Dodgers and drink sake
So you can't blame me
For loving cinema or imagination
And top mountain oxygen
A dream within a dream is
A faucet and a fountain
Said my friend the plumber
So who really cares if you're
A Kardashian or Darth Vader?
As long as you're at the screening
With an open mind and a Monster
In your pocket
Or on your knee

## ON VERDE

There are several leading
Luminaries who have commented
On how left handed citizens
Think, feel, and vote

I have not
Being more concerned
With looming deadly viruses and other such
Izquierdas
However, I cannot argue with these
Derechos borrachos
I am, in fact, in
The garden with Lorca
Right now

Forever
A concept he and I were discussing at
Fort Knox
Last September

Right before the Earth
Wind and Fire concert
During which several of our collaborative
Manuscripts were burned to a crisp
Bringing impermanence to the forefront
So to speak

Some of you, and I appreciate the chuckles, might believe…

Lorca's eyebrows raised
A series of flowerbeds (nards)
Gypsy romances & blood weddings
Poured from his ears—
Five years in an instant
Five instants in a year
A language for roses or marauders or
Lorcas
Upon Lorcas upon
Lorcas
On Lorcas
Four Lorcas in the deck
Five Lorcas from the palm of the hand
Six Lorcas in the shadow of Spain
Seven Lorcas in
The villages of Víznar and Alfacar

*Seven Brides for Seven Lorcas*
All yelling "Albondigas!"
Brings us to Buenos Aires in 1933

Sorry, I just can't stop saying "Lorcas"
And maybe I need to say it again
But when I think of Lorca
I think of no need to apologize

## ON VERDE II

There are several leading
Luminaries who have commented
On how left handed citizens
Think, feel, and vote

I have not
Being more concerned
With looming deadly viruses and other such
Izquierdas
However, I cannot argue with these
Derechos borrachos
I am, in fact, in
The garden with Lorca
Right now

Forever
A concept he and I were discussing at
Fort Knox
Last September

Right before the Earth
Wind and Fire concert
During which several of our collaborative
manuscripts were burned to a crisp
Bringing impermanence to the forefront
So to speak

Some of you, and I appreciate the chuckles, might believe…

Lorca's eyebrows raised
A series of flowerbeds (nards)
Gypsy romances & blood weddings
Poured from his ears—
Five years in an instant
Five instants in a year
A language for roses or marauders or
Lorcas
Upon Lorcas upon
Lorcas
On Lorcas
Four Lorcas in the deck
Five Lorcas from the palm of the hand
Six Lorcas in the shadow of Spain
Seven Lorcas in
The villages of Víznar and Alfacar

Seven Brides for Seven Lorcas
All yelling "Albondigas!"
Brings us to Buenos Aires in 1933

Sorry, I just can't stop saying "Lorcas"
And maybe I need to say it again
But when I think of Lorca
I think of no need to apologize

## 5 MINUTES TO MIDNIGHT

5 minutes to midnight
He writes in a poem
To his friend
Like a letter

That cannot be opened
Sitting on a shelf
In a wastebasket

Shitting on an elf
Next to a trophy
Under a spider

Satan's little helper
A veritable Eminem
Though every relationship seems the same

In the eyes of the spider
She writes this above him

She writes this inside him
She lays beside him

She lays inside him
A golden egg
That can never be opened

Only cracked
Like a letter

Unread
On New Year's Day

Sitting on a shelf
With an answer he knew all along

John Silver's
Baby back ribs

Inside a self
On a sign

Which seems to say
What every billboard wants you to know
"Eat or be eaten"

Or be Spider-Man
Or Aquaman
Forget about the self
Forget about everything, really

So—did you forget how to forget?
Is that why you're here?

Is this why we're having this discussion?
The words fell from the bottom of his trousers
Like a ton of chocolate muffins
And he stooped low enough to peer from his window onto the seaside below

Yep: bell-bottoms
He thought
An entire world
An entire life
In an instant
With just a glance
If he had only been
Made of pearls
Or given a sash that said Best Person
Or a vanilla muffin
Maybe all this business in Malta would vanish
Like a vanilla malt in Spanish
Or a yoga mat in Silver Lake
The billboards still above them
The billabongs
Below
Letters cracked and peeling

A brand-new blonde afro
A conditioner for a trapeze artist

By the name of Johnny Kafka

He was the last of the great equestrians
Back when people went to the circus
Back when people
Back when people
And just like that
Santa's little coprophiliac
Raises his shattered eyebrows

Back when people had
Had each other's backs
There was a sense of camaraderie

Not to mention a sense of hot-rod-erie
Drag races and whatnot
A big red man in drag holding a handkerchief

In one hand and an Indian Chief in the other
Each time someone thought they had caught her mariposa
She would shout a series of metaphors for how large her nose was

For example
"My nose is like an avalanche"
And the bystander who had hoped to sting
Would be left barbed, as empty as

A nose without snot
A rope without a noose

Amos without Andy
A moose on the loose
"My nose is like a red-hot caboose"
She could continue like this ad infinitum
A way of hiding their doomed fiefdom

Do you know what it's like to be everything?
To feel every fold in the cosmos?
I didn't stay a word

Like a letter
I folded myself
Into the envelope of our bed
Pulled out a stamp
Licked my forehead

And read what I wrote
To the future:

"I must become the future
Said the Historian to the Past"

To which the Past responded

## ACKNOWLEDGMENTS

Thanks to *New Orleans Review* for publishing the following poems:

"My Edits"
"Poem About Math"
"In the Catbird Seat"

LOREN GOODMAN is the author of *Famous Americans*, selected by W.S. Merwin for the 2002 Yale Series of Younger Poets, and *Non-Existent Facts* (otata's bookshelf, 2018), as well as the chapbooks *Suppository Writing* (The Chuckwagon, 2008) and *New Products* (Proper Tales Press, 2010). He is an Associate Professor of Creative Writing and English Literature at Yonsei University/Underwood International College in Seoul, Korea, and serves as the UIC Creative Writing Director.

✿

PIROOZ KALAYEH is a filmmaker, artist, and author. His films include *Shoplifting from American Apparel*, *The Human War*, *Brad Warner's Hardcore Zen*, *Zombie Bounty Hunter M.D.*, and *Ctrl Alt Del*. His novel *The Whopper Strategies* details an advertising executive's journey to package Enlightenment in a Box. His sixth feature *Sometimes I Dream in Farsi* is currently in post-production with ILIKENIRVANA Productions.

✿

COLOPHON

Text is set in a digital version of Jenson, designed by Robert Slimbach in 1996, and based on the work of punchcutter, printer, and publisher Nicolas Jenson. The titles here are in Futura.

❧

NEW MICHIGAN PRESS, based in Tucson, Arizona, prints poetry and prose chapbooks, especially work that transcends traditional genre. Together with DIAGRAM, NMP sponsors a yearly chapbook competition.

DIAGRAM, a journal of text, art, and schematic, is published bimonthly at THEDIAGRAM.COM. Periodic print anthologies are available from the New Michigan Press at NEWMICHIGANPRESS.COM.

www.ingramcontent.com/pod-product-compliance
Lightning Source LLC
Chambersburg PA
CBHW031501040426
42444CB00007B/1169